HOW TO

TEACH YOUR

<u>CHILDREN</u>

ABOUT

RACISM

(A letter from a Black Mother to White Parents)

UCHENNA L. UMEH, MD, MBA

A.K.A. DR. LULU | THE MOMATRICIAN

First Edition
How to Teach Your Children About Racism
by Uchenna L. Umeh, MD, MBA
a.k.a Dr. Lulu | The Momatrician

by Dr. Lulu®
11844 Bandera Rd, #723 Helotes TX 78023

www.teenalive.com
www.youthmotivationalspace.com
www.uchennaumeh.com

For permissions contact publisher: askdoctorlulu@gmail.com
Book Cover by Noble Daniel nobledaniel104@gmail.com

ISBN: 978-1-7337512-5-4

Table of Contents

"Racism is much like a malignant cancer, and America is the patient."

~Dr. Lulu

Dedication

I am calling this book my pivot book.

I interrupted the completion of a different book to write it.

It was borne out of pain and sadness following the death of George Floyd.

I am dedicating it to his memory, and to the memory of all Black people who have died in police custody, or from police brutality.

All those who have been killed, murdered, lynched, falsely prosecuted, and incarcerated.

All those who have been discriminated against across the globe in the name of racism.

May your souls and spirits find resting peace.

"No other life matters
until all Black lives matter."

~ Dr. Lulu

Thank you for your purchase!

This is your FREE GIFT!

Are you a parent?

Here is a list of some fun activities for you and your kids.

Type the following link onto your browser.

https://bit.ly/37GqL57

Enjoy!

The people, places and events described on the following pages are real. For a more in-depth explanation of some of the names and phrases used, please see the appendix at the back of this book.

Acknowledgements

The idea of this book came out of pain, suffering, and death. I would like to thank Christian Cooper and the families of George Floyd, Ahmaud Arbery and Breaona Taylor. Without their sacrifice and pain, it would never have been written.

I would like to specifically thank my sons. You inspire me daily. You make me feel all the ranges of emotions possible for a mother to feel. I thank you for choosing to come into this world through me. No greater love.

A huge thank you goes to my Facebook family and friends. You awakened something in me with your response to my original blog post. Many thanks, in particular, to the one lady whose comment was, "This would make a great book."

My beta readers, my book cover designer, my crowdsourcing family, and my launch team. You are all magic. I called and you responded. You made this book happen. I remain loyal and grateful.

For everyone who will read this book, thank you for letting my words into your hearts. I pray they find a soft landing, spring roots, and bear much fruit. This is only the beginning. There's much work to be done. Thank you for joining us in the vineyard.

Other Books by Uchenna L. Umeh, MD, MBA

1) How to Raise Well-Rounded Children
2) A Teen's Life

In the Works

1) What if My Child is A Bully?

Praise for How to Teach Your Children About Racism

"I implemented just one of Dr. Lulu's commandments, and like magic I could see the empathy shine through my child's eyes. No parent wants their child to be a racist" ~ Ali N

"Wonderful!!! Well-articulated and presented. This book will not only be another bestseller, but also an award-winning one. Bravo and congratulations! ~ Ngozi U

"Amazing book! So excited for you and this book!!! Excellent content, and very much needed!!!" ~ Christina D

"I can comfortably state that White America has been kneeling on our necks from the days of slavery until now"

~ Dr. L

Chapter 1

Ruminating on My Thoughts

Dear White-American Parents,

I have a few questions. Are you comfortable in your White skin? Would you ever want your kids, relatives or even yourself to be treated the way Black people in America are treated? If you wouldn't, then that means you know it happens, and perhaps are not doing anything about it. If you are doing something about it, then this letter might not be for you. But if you would like to change the way things currently are, then continue reading.

I don't know about you, but, the past several months (March through June of 2020) have been extremely challenging for me. It has been one of those times in my life when I feel like I am in the twilight zone. It appears all the things going on around me are surreal. If anyone had told me that the year 2020 was going to be like this by only June, I would have never believed them. In American terms, I would ask for my money back.

We have gone from a "Happy New Year" to a weird Spring, to an even weirder Summer. There is racial tension in the air, not only in the United States, but joining us in solidarity, nearly every nation of our earth has participated in protests. I have never in my 50+ years experienced anything like this. While I am glad that the world is *"uniting"* for once to fight a for cause, this cause is however, as old, and as deep-rooted as the blood that runs through our veins.

First off, Black America lost Kobe Bryant in January. Then came a pandemic with a mandatory lockdown and an entire production that has been shrouded in conspiracy. One that has resulted in the deaths of hundreds of thousands of people across the globe. It is disproportionately claiming the lives of thousands of Black people, particularly in America. These untimely deaths result from significant health disparities stemming from intentional, systematic, and sustained institutionalized racism.

As everyone knows, the quarantine and lockdown lasted for about 8 to 10 weeks. It was initially unbelievable that the entire world would be on lockdown for an indefinite duration of time. But for the most part, we all started getting used to it. And getting used to the fact that the world as we know it will probably never be the same again. Then it started. The news of Ahmaud Arbery hit the airwaves, then Breaona Taylor, then Christian Cooper, then George Floyd. Sadly, there are many, many, many more names that might remain unknown. Too numerous to be mentioned in this book.

I probably don't need to repeat everything that's happened in recent times here. Suffice it to say that racism in America, police brutality and the nonsense killings of unarmed Black people finally jumped on the world's stage for everyone to see. There is a Nigerian adage that goes, *"it is good for the wind to expose what lies hidden under the feathers of a rooster's tail."* Essentially saying, that what is done in the dark, will eventually come to the light.

Black people in America have endured racism and all forms of discrimination for far too long. Luckily or unluckily, the entire world watched a murder play out this one time. Thankfully, people are joining in protesting against the sustained systematic racism and discrimination against mainly Black people across the globe.

For those of us living in the United States, we have now come face to face with the reality of our poor, no, sorry state of race relations. Even if you don't live in the United States, you are no longer able to say you *"don't know."* You can neither claim ignorance of its presence nor oblivion of the full extent of its dangers. As a parent coach, I will try to educate you the best way that I can. I already started that in my first book: "How to Raise Well Rounded Children" (Amazon).

Police brutality, modern-day lynching, or White people calling the police on Black people going about their business, has caused every single Black person in the United States, to remain in a perpetual state of fear for their safety. We are overwhelmed, wondering what exactly is going on, and watching it repeatedly play out with little or no resulting consequences for the perpetrators.

Lying awake one night, I was ruminating on my thoughts and wondering what I could do to help with creating awareness. I was trying to protect my family, remain safe, sane, and vigilant. As a pediatrician and mom, I felt I needed to do something that would tie them all together. Something different. Something practical. Something real.

I figured some White people might need guidance and simple rules to follow. Some of you have reached out to me asking what you can do to help. I am guessing that being an immigrant, I have enough to say and I will be speaking from my heart. Besides, my sons, friends, and family members have all been victims of racism. So, I decided to put together these 21 commandments to help guide you.

Chapter 2

Definition

Racism is defined by most dictionaries, as a belief system that race is the primary determinant of human traits and capacities. That racial differences produce an inherent superiority of a race (White) over another race (in my case, Black). Or that groups of humans possess different behavioral traits corresponding to physical appearance. And they can be divided based on the superiority of one race over another.

Racism can also be defined as prejudice, discrimination, hatred, or antagonism directed against someone of a different race. These are primarily based on the belief that one's own race is superior. In other words, no matter how you look at it, racism is about the superiority or inferiority of races. The most disturbing fact is that it is 100% man-made. Yep, *racism is exclusively practiced by humans.*

To be clear, the acts of racism and the mindset of supremacy, White supremacy, can only be practiced *unidirectionally*. It is often demonstrated by certain members of one race towards *every member* of the other race. In other words, one Black man mistreating one White man is *not* an act of racism. There are no systems in place to encourage the behavior or to enforce it.

However, the rules and processes in place in the United States, allow White people to consistently mistreat Black people. Quite often with little or no repercussions. Many of them believe it is their right to do so. They were literally raised to believe that Black people equate to less than their house-hold pets, other animals, or lower.

Did you know that racism and prejudice are fundamentally rooted in fear and ignorance? This fear often comes from a lack of knowledge or understanding of who Black people really are, and how we came to be in the United States. This ignorance then leads to fear, fear leads people to draw the wrong conclusions, and those conclusions become their truth. Then that "truth" is passed down from generation to generation as binding falsehoods and concepts like "*all Black men are a threat.*" It then becomes a system and a way of doing things.

Chapter 3

A Quick Background

I am a Nigerian immigrant. My sons were born and bred in the United States. They are bona fide African Americans, but in this book, I shall refer to all of us as Black people. My sons do not know any other home, and every member of my family has experienced some form of racism.

I come from a country where there is only one race and different tribes, and I must admit I have experienced ethnicism and tribalism. While they are also forms of prejudice, their differences are beyond the scope of this book.

In contrast, since living in the United States, I have encountered racism numerous times. At the workplace, on the train, from my neighbors, at the airport, and during Mass in the Catholic Church. I have experienced it while shopping at the mall or at the grocery store, at the drycleaners and while taking a walk on the green way.

It has even happened at the restaurant, the car-rental, bank, movies, and while sitting and chilling in my backyard.

The racism has been nonstop, but each time I have experienced it in the past, I have gone with the flow. You see, for me, I know deep inside that most of my perpetrators are either jealous, insecure, or act out of contempt. But, when it happened to my sons recently, naturally, my reaction was very different.

My sons take turns walking our dog Lulu, every evening. *Every time* they walk out the door, I say the words *"make sure you come back."* One day, my last son asked me why I always say those words. I had to explain to him that *"Trayvon Martin never came back home from walking to the corner store."* For me it is a constant worry. I never get a chance to take a break. There is no such thing as *"he just went around the corner."*

He could even be playing in the backyard and get shot by the police. The same people who have sworn to serve and protect him. In the eyes of America, once he leaves my house, he immediately becomes *"a threat"* because of the color of his skin. Both the police and any White person who owns a gun and is in the mood to shoot a Black man that day can kill him. They don't need a reason. Or he might have the police called on him by a White woman who feels *"threatened."* Even if she is breaking the law as she walks her dog in a park.

As fate would have it, recently, my fears were realized one evening when my eldest and my youngest sons went running together in our neighborhood. I usually insist they accompany each other for my own sanity. As soon as they walked back into the house, I knew right away that something had happened. My youngest son finally spoke up and told me a White police officer in a marked cruiser had followed them home.

As upset as I was that night, I realized that I truly couldn't do anything about it. I was *helpless*. That fact hit me hard, and I wept silently for my boys. I shook my head and lowered it in disbelief as I whispered a silent *thank you* to the universe. We have lived in this home for 8 years. My sons went to school here. Everyone else strolls or runs in the neighborhood, but my sons were singled out and profiled.

I always shudder as I ask myself what if the police officer had stopped them? What if he had been in a bad mood? What if it happens again? We live in Texas, it could even happen to me, anyone remember Sandra Bland? Google her if unsure. Sadly, as I write this, my eldest son will not go out to run anymore. He is scared. He is scarred. A young life should not be lived this way.

Black boys and girls should never live in fear. Black parents should never have worry about their children or themselves not returning home. My eldest son turned 22 years old on the 29th of

May, but he refused to celebrate his birthday. He was mourning the death of George Floyd only a few days prior.

I, on the other hand, worry about the reality that this might be his last birthday. What if someone somewhere decides to be threatened by his mere presence as a Black man, and chooses to kill him? What if he goes out and never comes home one day? What if, what if…?

I also weep for George Floyd's little daughter who will grow up without the love of her doting father. He will not be there to father her. He will not get to drop her off at school. She will not get to attend her father and daughter school dance with him. He will not get to share her prom with her. He will never get to walk her down the aisle. Neither he nor I will be able to protect our kids, but *you* can.

You see, Black parents live with a constant and present fear about their children's safety. We have endured pain and suffering from way back in the days of slavery. The discussion about slavery is beyond the scope of this book, however, the pain of the enslavement of our ancestors is forever with us. It *never* goes away.

It is something that has become ingrained in our hearts. It is something we can pass on to our children through Transgenerational Trauma or Epigenetics. A process whereby a mother can transmit her pain to her offspring at birth or while rearing them, but not through her genes. It is the cause of Post Traumatic Slave Syndrome (PTSS), or Persistent Traumatic Stress Disorder (PTSD), or Post Traumatic Stress Disorder (PTSD).

It is exhausting. It is traumatizing, and it is an unhealthy state of mind for me, and other Black parents like me. These concepts cause a sense of a shortened lifespan, and increase the risk of suicide in Black people. I know this because I write and speak about youth suicide. A topic I discuss at length in my second book, A Teen's Life (Amazon).

Most people are unaware that Black children aged 5 through 12 years are twice as likely as their White counterparts to die by suicide. The fact has been repeatedly proven by multiple studies that have yielded the same result. A 2018 article by The Washington Post details the results. They were published in the Pediatrics Journal of American Medical Association (JAMA Pediatrics). Unfortunately, the suicide phenomenon extends through their teen and adult years.

Chapter 4

Start the Conversation: Light the Spark

Racism, much like Black trauma can also be handed down through the generations. Sadly, many White people today are in disbelief of this fact. Partially because it has always been their way of life, and partially because they may never have thought about it. Many of you will not admit to the concept of "White Supremacy," yet you capitalize on your "White Privilege."

Yeah, I know, the conversation about race is one that some White families have never had, but obviously need to. While families like mine hold conversations about racism nearly every day, many other families have never even thought about it. I often say I will light the spark. Today, however, I want you to light the spark and start the conversation.

It must start. The time is now. Things must begin to change. As the first teachers of children, parents are in the driver's seat. We have the power to begin the process of making the much-needed change in our world. We are witnessing how dangerous it is to be *"color blind"* or *"color neutral."* It is time to be *"color brave."* It is also time to listen, and to have an open mind. Yes, *it is time to listen.*

Listening rather than speaking or complaining and getting frustrated will entail you stepping out of your comfort zone. It will require you embarking on a journey to literally unlearn everything you have learned. Ignorance and inaction have brought us to this historical point in our world today. To do that, you will need my 3Es: *Empathy*, *Effort*, and *Education.*

Empathy for Black people. This is critical, but even more critical, is developing and practicing *Compassion* for the entire Black race. For centuries, we have not had a fair opportunity to thrive in America. Empathy is defined as the ability to understand and share the feelings of another. Compassion takes it up a notch to include kindness, and the willingness to *help* others.

White America needs a healthy dose of a combination of both character traits. It also needs to include its offspring in the journey towards their daily practice. To arrive at your destination, you must go from a state of unconscious bias, to a completely unbiased state in everything you do concerning us.

Effort on your part. Effort to do everything you need to do to *not* be a racist, and to *actively* be anti-racist. That means becoming comfortable with having uncomfortable discussions with your friends, family members and colleagues. That means becoming a true ally, with the real possibility of losing friends or becoming estranged from family members.

Change will require *sustained* effort. That means waking up every morning and doing everything in your power to fight racism in all facets of your life. It will be tough, but it is doable. Like everything worthwhile, it starts from within you. You must be the change. Never have those words had a truer meaning than now.

Education. For this, you need to get very familiar and acquainted with the who, the why, the what, the when and the how of racism. Remember those famous five? Yup, we need to go back to them. Find books, movies, articles, documentaries, milk bottles or shoe boxes. Find people, family members, or friends. Find anything and anyone who will have information about slavery, including, perhaps, your own family history.

In addition, you must be ready to impart all the amassed knowledge onto your children. Your family and your friends might need it too. We shall discuss this in a bit more detail in the commandments section of this book. Remember, I am not blaming you for racism. I am simply sharing my knowledge and my thoughts and fears with you.

Chapter 5

What is My Point?

I can comfortably state that White America has been kneeling on our necks from the days of slavery until now. You see, what happened to George Floyd, can literally only happen in America. For over four hundred years, Black people in America have continued to suffer in all aspects of our lives.

We have been discriminated against, frustrated, and literally been hunted like wild animals. It is torture. We have no respite. Not at home, not at work, not at play, not anywhere. At work for instance, we are expected to work more than twice as hard to be recognized less than half as much. The dehumanization must stop! Those who are silent now, or continue to be, *must* examine their why.

Some much-needed soul-searching should be on everyone's to-do list now! Black lives not only matter, they are also worthy, they are loved, and they are needed. That does not mean all other lives do not matter. It simply means that as of now, today, Black lives *need* mattering, because for far too long, they have *not* mattered. Until ***all Black lives matter***, no other lives can ever really matter.

Sadly, our children are caught in the crossfire. I recently posed the following question on my Facebook page: What would happen if we put 10 children in a room for 10 minutes? The answers I received from my friends were as interesting as they were different. The truth is, the kids will start playing with each other right away. No judgement.

If the same experiment was performed on grown-ups, they will more than likely say nothing to each other. They might reluctantly speak, but with caution. Given enough time, they will eventually team up according to some categories, preconceptions, or misconceptions about each other.

The males together, the Black people together, the Nigerians together, the Blue collars together, you get my point. The question is, how did we arrive at that? Why and how do we go from playing together in the sandbox at age four to barely looking at each other at age forty?

Inspired by a Facebook post that a friend of mine tagged me on, I decided to write the original blog article (see my blog in the Appendix of this book) that led to the idea of this book. I wrote it because I am doing my part to create a healthier *racism-free* world for my children to live and thrive in. I also wrote it to follow my own advice. To educate people with basic knowledge of the real situation of things in my home.

My guess is the same applies to many Black homes across the United States and the world at large. Racism is indeed the proverbial elephant in the room, and thus must be tackled. So, here are my commandments on how to approach *the talk about racism* with your young'uns. Enjoy! Let me know what you think. Feel free to contact me via my email, askdoctorlulu@gmail.com

Chapter 6

The 21 Commandments

1) **Thou shalt first become comfortable with having uncomfortable conversations with thyself, before ever trying to have them with any other person.**

In today's America, we are experiencing consequences and vicarious trauma from the recent murders of unarmed Black people by White men. At this point, you must get into that space of vulnerability and face your fears and insecurities. It is needed in order to deal with the harsh reality of unchecked years of racism.

If you are uncomfortable talking about it, dig deep and figure out why you are. You can only get past that point with intention, mindfulness and focus. Allow yourself some grace knowing this might be harder than you expect, but be willing and determined to stay the course. This will not be the hardest conversation you will ever have, but it will make the cut on the list of the top 3. So, put your best foot forward and lead with your heart, it can be done.

2) Thou shalt educate thyself appropriately. Gather all the facts that thou might need and yet not have, before embarking on any discussions with thy children.

Children are smart, they ask the darndest questions, they say the darndest things. They will see through your charade. They are already learning about it, hearing about it, or talking about it in their little cliques and group chats. Is the topic of racism a taboo in your home? If so, your child might have questions, but might not ask because they are scared or not sure how to approach you.

Since you might have to bring up the topic, you might as well be their guide. Be casual, take it easy, start with a general intro like the pandemic, and all the "stuff" that has been happening. Then get more specific on exactly what it is you are referring to.

I know that talking about race can be sensitive, and maybe even a bit messy, but the other option is *not* an option. My advice is to just buckle up and do it. Oh, and please don't expect Black people to educate you on what exactly to say. You have full and likely better access to the same sources of information that we have. Please know that asking us to teach you is an extra burden when we are the ones in need of support.

3) **Thou shalt ensure that thy abode is *anti-racist*. Remember, information can be conveyed by thoughts, words or deeds, and thy children will absorb them all from thee.**

I cannot say enough that charity begins at home, but anti-racist behavior begins in your heart, because that is your real *"home."* As the saying goes, *"from the abundance of the heart, the mouth speaketh."* So, by abode, I mean both your physical house as well as the home inside the four chambers of your heart.

You will need to embark upon an appropriate soul-searching journey for that to occur. That move should be front and center now. This might be a time when you need to start the practice of *mindfulness* and to be *intentional* and *present* in every moment of your parenting.

Do you know that your heart, your words, and your actions might be racist, and you might not even be aware of it? Rest assured, your kids will watch you, absorb it, master it, and begin to practice it. By then it might be too late to unlearn the bad lessons. Remember, today is the first day of the rest of your life, so start today, start now, start with this book. Your mind must be expunged of all racist thoughts that reside there.

4) Thou shalt first find out from thy children what they already know about racism before proceeding with the teaching.

A simple question and answer session will suffice. I also love storytelling, so, you could begin with that before the Q and A. You may use any of the stories on White on Black killing in circulation now. Have you ever acted out of prejudice? You could share that personal experience, one that you witnessed, or you were a part of. Or one that you could have prevented but did not.

I told you to get comfortable with discomfort. I also told you it would not be easy, but if you have an open communication line with your children, then it might be that much easier.

There is no point in building a house upon a faulty foundation. First, dig up the old one (find out what the kids know), then proceed with laying new earth and building blocks (teaching them new things). You might be pleasantly surprised at how well your kids will receive the information. Furthermore, this process might be easier in the end if you approach it from a *"right versus wrong"* perspective. Go ahead, I am cheering you on.

5) Thou shalt start to teach thy children about systematic, systemic, and institutional racism as early as they can understand.

Did you know that as early as six months a baby's brain can notice race-based differences? Did you know that kids can begin to internalize racial biases by ages two to four? By the age of seven, most children know right from wrong. By the age of twelve, they are already set in their ways.

Being their parent, you should already know your child, and know exactly what they can and cannot understand as they get older. This means you should start teaching them about the practice of systemic racism as early as they can understand. Teach them how to identify and fight it before the end of their first decade of life.

With *intention* and *mindfulness*, explain the following concepts:
*Redlining
*Mass incarceration
*Police brutality
*Racial profiling
*Housing inequality
*Segregation
*Lynching
*Population displacement
*Healthcare disparities
*Gentrification
*School to prison pipeline

This list is not exhaustive, but it is a start. They are all tough topics to discuss, but this will go a long way in the long run.

6) Thou shalt use words like "we," "us," and "our" when having these conversations with thy children.

I think it is important to identify with or insert yourself into the storylines you will be telling your children. Rather than phrases like *"some people are bad,"* or *"some people are racists,"* use phrases like *"people like us, White people,"* or *"people that look like mom and dad or grandpa and grandma."*

Say *"we have done bad or mean things."* Or *"we have been mistreating, discriminating, killing, or murdering people like* (enter names of Black kids they know). Or simply come out and say, *"people like us killed George Floyd."*

Ensure you explain exactly why these people are being killed in these modern-day lynching, *"the color of their skin."* I know that this whole process will need a lot of getting used-to, but it is the most transparent and honest thing you can do. In my opinion, it is the very best way to do it, so, own it.

7) Thou shalt expose thy children to other cultures, by visiting their museums, their churches, or attending civic events organized by them.

There is no better way to begin your journey of getting immersed into <u>African American</u>, <u>Jewish</u>, <u>Native American</u>, <u>Hispanic</u> or any other different ethnicity's history than by doing this. Visit their museums, civic centers, places of worship, or one of the many events these cultural communities often hold in a city near you. Not being able to go in person because of the physical distancing for the pandemic is not an excuse.

The internet will help you. A simple Google search will suffice. There are also many virtual online events taking place now. Every one of us is spending an inordinate amount of time online these days. You might as well carve out time to spend with your young'uns surfing the internet and learning together. The time is now! While Summer is always a good time for such activities, don't wait for summer, just, put on your masks and get going!

8) **Thou shalt endeavor to cook, order-in, or learn about foods of other ethnicities**.

This is a must! Humans are social beings. We love to eat. It is what we do. I believe this is one basic human activity that every race and every person partake in. We get together to eat and drink whether the going is good or bad, it is the human way. We also tend to let down our guards when we are eating, to talk.

In my home, my family has rotated the same international menu for dinner for over 15 years. Take a look at our weekly menu and a few examples.

Mondays; **Italian** (Pizza, Spaghetti)

Tuesdays; **American** (Burgers, Chicken & Broccoli)

Wednesdays; **Mexican** (Tacos, Enchiladas)

Thursdays; **Nigerian** (Pounded Yam with Bitter-leaf soup, Jollof Rice and Plantain)

Fridays; **Chinese** (House Fried Rice, Gen Tso Chicken)

Saturdays and Sundays; Miscellaneous/Leftovers

For the most part, many Americans I have met like to try new things, so why not try new foods? You would do that if you traveled to my country wouldn't you? Never mind the lady on the *90 Day Fiancé* television show 😊.

So, when next you visit your "Nigerian friend" perhaps (wink wink), ask about...

*_fufu_ ati _efo riro_ (swallow and soup)

*_jollof rice_ with *"shikin"* (cook-up rice)

*_dodo_ (fried plantains)

*_isiewu_ (goat head delicacy)

*_ofensal_a (fish pepper soup)

 *_nkwobi_ (cow foot delicacy)

These are all tasty mouth-watering meals that you can only enjoy by having an open mind. Take it from me, they are all very *#delish*, you will love them!

I for one, love to try new things, and new foods tops that list. I also enjoy listing out and explain the ingredients, and the process of creating various dishes whenever I host parties.

9) Thou shalt listen to music and learn dance moves from other cultures…yes, thou must!

Okay, I know, I told you to have an open mind, remember? While I wouldn't necessarily ask you to learn the acrobatic *nkpokiti*, or the popular <u>break-dancing</u> from the glorious 90s, it is certainly time to move on from your line-dancing ways to something new, different, fun, and exposes a whole new world to you.

Your kids will love the moves, the melody, and the novelty. They can brag about their new skills to their friends. This could also be a bonding exercise for y'all. Besides, while we are all still under a semi-quarantine, introducing a new activity like dancing will certainly add spice and break up the monotony of staying at home. It might even ward off some of the boredom your teens and tweens are currently experiencing.

10) Thou shalt endeavor to learn a foreign language, preferably a language native to Africa. Thou shalt also teach said language to thy offspring or learn it together.

Yes, spread your wings, fly far away to the land of spoken word, communication and understanding. To the land of open-mindedness and love. To the land of knowledge and power. Because learning our "language," verbal or nonverbal, spoken words and unspoken words, will empower you and help you better understand us as a people.

Once you understand, there will be no more fear, and when there is no fear, there is no racism. One practice I have is, when I walk into an immigrant patient's room, I immediately greet them in their own native language: *"Hola," "Bonjour," "Salaam alaikum,"* etc.

That seemingly insignificant move breaks away all barriers, visible and invisible. Right away their guards and defenses are laid down. They immediately let me into their circle. I become their friend, their ally, someone they *can* trust with their ailment. It is powerful.

11) **Thou shalt encourage thy children to make friends with, and visit homes of children of other races, and have them visit thy home in return**.

Okay, I admit, this one would likely be the most challenging of the lot. With the tension in the air it might be a bit tricky, *but it can be done!* One thing I know about children is, they are not born racists. They acquire racism as they grow up, and I might add, they learn it from you, their parents.

With that in mind, I will ask you to allow your children to make friends with children of other races. You should make a concerted effort to encourage them to do so. Get to know these friends' parents and learn a thing or two about their history and upbringing. Extend a hand of friendship.

Offer to take their kids to a game, pick them up from school or even buy them dinner. Get out of your comfort zone a bit, and with practice, it will get better. Once the quarantine is over, and we can get back to doing things the way we used to, a visit to the park or the pool might be a great icebreaker.

12) Thou must become acutely aware of the microaggression some things thou doeth or sayeth can cause to people like me.

Like calling me the nurse or "miss" when my name tag clearly says MD. Or asking me where I went to medical school, how I came to America (Yes, I was asked that when I lived in South Carolina). Or wondering how my English is *so good*. Or not trying at all to pronounce my name after I have told you how to say it…more than once.

I don't really like it when you comment on my accent (like you don't have one). Or ask to touch my hair to *"know what it feels like."* Or marveling when I tell you that I speak 7 languages (I am working on my 8th, Mandarin). Or assuming that I am a wait staff, rather than a patron at the restaurant. Or that my sons attend college on a basketball scholarship! I could go on and on, but you get the drift.

If you asked any Black person (especially an immigrant) in America, you would get an earful of their own experiences. My suggestion is to stop and think before you ask a question or say something. Oh, and should you ever find yourself wondering if a question or a statement might be racist? *It most likely is.*

13) **Thou shalt police thyself, thy relatives, and thy children with purpose, intention, and mindfulness.**

As bad as police brutality is, it is only a lead point, one of the multitudes of symptoms of racism. It is not the main problem itself. Racism spans a whole gamut (see commandment #5 above) and should be approached as such, from multiple lead points.

While police brutality is the main course on the menu now, my concerns also include those non-uniformed men and women who are out there. The seemingly invisible ones who feel a need to kill the Ahmaud Arberys and Trayvon Martins of the world. The cowards who are lynching Black men in public places in 2020 and *calling them suicides.*

You must ensure that you are not perpetuating intolerance, hate, or prejudice in any way. You know your friends and family members who are racist. You must be bold, act, and police them. *Speak up.* We are tired of being tired of being tired. You must have *"the talk"* with these people. And if they still *choose* to be silent, or continue the behavior, then I suggest you re-evaluate your relationship with them.

To become a true ally, you must be willing to cut off the parts of you that wish to remain on the other side. I never said this was going to be easy, but you are either with us wholly, or you are not. You cannot have it both ways. While it is not necessarily *us versus them*, it is however, *you versus your conscience, your heart, and your soul.*

14) Thou shalt visit the predominantly Black parts of the city or town thou liveth in…with thy children in tow.

Let's get this straight, I am not asking you to send your child to a Historically Black College or University (HBCU). I am simply asking you to take a short trip to our neighborhoods. Get to see what life is like over here. Just a visit. You might begin to gain a bit of clarity, empathy, compassion, understanding, and maybe even respect.

You need them to begin your journey towards avoiding racism and more importantly, becoming anti-racist. For too long we have been divided and separated geographically. This has worsened the divide in our hearts as well.

The time is now for you to start doing what it takes, by becoming proactive in your homes. Your daughter(s) want to date our son(s), that is a fact. You might as well get to know where they hang out /will be hanging out all summer. You never know, it might lead to us serving soul-food at the wedding, so get ready 😊

15) Thou shalt teach thy child to recognize bullying behavior and speak up wherever it occurs, especially at school.

Most people do not realize that racism is a form of bullying. Bullying requires the following: a power in-balance, repetition, intent to harm, a bully, a victim, and a bystander. If you examine the treatment of Black people in America over the past four hundred years, you will see a clear picture of bullying, except it is on the largest scale ever.

Bullying is a catalyst for suicide in children, and as we know, it is a HUGE problem in our schools. My next book happens to be on bullying, "What If My Child Is A Bully?" Stay tuned, it is coming soon on Amazon. As a former victim of bullying, I implore you to educate your kids about it. Ask them to find the kids who are victimized and sit with them on the school bus or at the cafeteria, or at the playground.

We know that many Black kids are bullied because of their race. They are called really mean names. Instruct your kids to befriend them and play with them at recess. They can also try to challenge the bullies and stand up to them. All that will go a long way towards ending the current epidemic of suicide in Black youth.

16) **Thou shalt not make a mockery or joke about any person who is different from thee on account of their race, and neither should thy offspring.**

It is imperative that as White parents, you raise your children to always see Black and Brown people in a good light. No one is asking for perfection here (because we all have our own forms of *implicit bias*). What I am asking is for you to start by simply *thinking* about Black people as equal humans.

We should all first be *humanists,* right? And I mean that in the simplest sense of the word. I believe the fancy name for that now is *"humanization."* Either way, America has so far been guilty of de-humanizing its Black and Brown citizens for far too long. So, please, be more sensitive with your jokes. Don't ridicule our skin tone, our kinky hair, our body type, or any other physical attribute that pertains to our race.

Don't engage in such with your kids. No one likes to be ridiculed. I always ask my patients' parents to imagine how they would feel if *their* child was ever the butt of the joke. What about *you*? How would *you* feel?

Did you know that mockery and teasing, aka verbal bullying is the most common form of bullying? It usually starts subtly, but, before you know it, it takes a life of its own, and then *things fall apart.*

17) Thou shalt not abuse thy White privilege by using it with an intent to harm.

Since this crisis begun, I have come to meet, know, and recognize the "Karens," "BBQ Beckys," and all their friends. Those who call "the Popo" on Black people going about their business, doing mundane things. Needless to add, this behavior has now become an epidemic.

I believe comedian/actress Niecy Nash named it "Wyt-Fear." Here is the problem though; each time you call the police, you are taking them away from their "more important work of policing." You are also potentially about to participate in killing that person whom you called the police on! *Stop that!*

There is no way to convince me that Amy Cooper did not fully understand what she was doing at the park in New York that fateful day. She knew all too well that the words *"an African American man is threatening my life"* would surely result in his death. She knew it, but she did it anyway. Use examples like that to teach your children about what *not* to do.

18) Thou shalt accept and embrace thy White privilege and use it for good, and only good.

As counter intuitive as these words are for me to write, they are necessary none-the-less. During the protests, my heart has been warmed each time I have seen pictures and videos of White protesters. Not those who incite violence, but those who laid face down on the ground between the police and the peaceful Black protesters.

Those who linked their arms and formed a human shield to protect the innocent. That is "positive" use of White privilege in action. If I could recommend any pictures or videos for you to share with your children, it would be those. Take your time to explain the differences in the pictures.

Explain the significance of these kinds of friends and allies and the long-term effects of such radical acts of selflessness on display. Doing so will not only teach your children how to *openly* not be racist, but also how to *fearlessly* be anti-racist. That is powerful. Many people don't know that they are two different concepts.

A couple of nights ago, a friend of mine shared a video with me. That video warmed my heart so much, that I reached out in gratitude to the lady who shot it. She is White. She and her husband pulled over and recorded an encounter between four policemen and a Black youth. In the video, the policemen made him sit in the median of a highway. After harassing him, they let him go.

The beautiful thing is the lady, her husband, and other good Samaritans all stayed and kept watch until the man was let go. She ended her post with #staywithmyson. That, and similar acts like that are what I am asking you to do. She didn't have to do that, but she did. She is a true angel. She was exemplifying the concept of "it takes a village to *save* a child."

I need you to be kind, and compassionate like her. When you see something, say something or better still, record it. I *love* her for that. That kid is home safe today, possibly because of heroes like her. What about you? Will you keep watch over my son? Will you be our hero? Will you make sure to #staywithmyson?

19) Thou shalt not justify thy racist behavior with Biblical or other religious teachings whatsoever!

This is critical! America was supposedly built on Christian principles, but we know that slavery was justified with words from the Bible. We know that lynching by certain extremist groups is also often justified with words from said holy book.

We even currently have a president who is endorsed by the Evangelicals. America for the most part is a country with practicing Christians. How do we justify these acts of terror and hate?

Here is the deal; if you truly believe that racism is bad, then you should not use the "good book" to justify it. If you believe that you are a good Christian, then you have no business perpetuating racism. Worst of all, allowing your child who comes pure and innocent from God, to learn of such practices from you.

That will almost guarantee you will not be taking a trip to the pearly gates after your time on this earth. Do the right thing, while you can. Our time here is finite. Moreover, you know I am right ☺

20) **Thou shalt be civil to thy Black co-workers, support Black-owned businesses, and donate to Black organizations when possible.**

This should not be too difficult. If you go about your business at work believing that everyone is equal and deserves a chance, you will not practice racism. If you discontinue seeing people soley based on the color of their skin, you will be good. You should return home each day and only say positive things about your co-workers, whatever skin color they are.

Be more attentive to this point especially if the co-workers are Black. Your children are watching your every move. They are learning from you. They will certainly repeat your words and actions to other people when you least expect it. Remember to be *consciously unbiased.*

It is also a great idea to support Black causes: Black owned businesses, Black organizations, and bail funds. Such funds as you know are to help people who have been (wrongfully) arrested and cannot afford bail. In America, many of them are Black.

You will also need to explain these things to your children. Get them to experience this form of kindness first-hand through you.

21) **Thou shalt ensure that all the above are adhered to, and from time to time, check in with thy child to assess for progress.**

Any good teacher knows to check in with their students from time to time. You will be no different. In addition, you must also continue to work on yourself and on your family members. The "Karens," "Beckys," "Amys," "Stephanies," "Dereks," "George's," "Gregorys," and "Travises." All these White people are now famous on the internet for either calling the police on innocent Black people, police brutality, or lynching.

There is much work to be done. Policing the police is not enough. We must also police ourselves, our thought processes and mindsets lest we remain imprisoned by them.

It is easy to spot the police like Derek Chauvin while in uniform or in their cruiser. It is, however, much harder to spot Karen or Gregory and Travis. They are dressed in the same clothes as you and me, but you *know* who they are, they are *your* family members.

They eat and drink, wine and dine, sleep, and wake up, and go to the place of worship with you.

Expose them. Take one for the team. Do it for the greater good. Though it might feel strange at the onset, it will all work out. You will feel good about doing the right thing, and you never know, they might come around because of you. Martin Luther King Jr. once said, *"The time is always right to do what is right."*

You could start right now by doing a small part to treat the Black people you meet in your daily lives with dignity and respect. I know that is not too much to ask.

Chapter 7

Lastly…

The entire world has now seen America in the true light. We see its racism manifest in all its ramifications. Countries all around the world now realize the deep rot that lies hidden at its core, in its heart, and deep within its soul. I know racism is not limited to America, but this is where I live. This is where my sons live. This is where my experiences were born.

Racism is much like a malignant cancer, and America is the star patient. ~ Dr. Lulu.

In its case, its cancer has metastasized and ravaged every aspect of its body. It is now dying a slow, insidious, and sure death. Like most patients with cancer, the prognosis is grim. We shall need more than a radical excision, radiotherapy, and chemotherapy. The treatment protocol must include *a change in diet, lifestyle, and a whole new and holistic process* to heal.

Sadly, I don't know that I shall live to see the needed changes take place. The situation is grave. It is deeply ingrained. Its literally woven into the fabric of the DNA of the United States of America. The self-proclaimed leader of the free world. Arguably one of the more "civilized" countries in the world. And the current leadership is fanning flames of division, rather than building bridges of hope.

I can only hope and pray that the winds of change are blowing. I must as a matter of necessity continue to watch my back and pray for my sons every day. Each time they leave my sight I will pray that the heavens and my ancestors will lead them safely home. I shall continue to do so, until I live out my natural life. That is the prayer of any mother. I hope it is your prayer for your children as well.

I will end by asking you to look at my face at the back of this book. It is the face of a woman, a mother who loves her sons. A woman who wants only what is best for them. A mother who would lay down her life for her children. I know you would do the same for yours.

I am a woman who just happens to be a Black person living in America. A woman who knows that the heart of man is wicked, but it is changeable. A woman who knows that our children are our future. They are the best *of* us. They are the best *in* us. In their eyes, we see their unborn children, our lineage, our next generation. The continuation of our bloodline.

Parents are not meant to bury their offspring, that is a fact of life. I have had enough of the untimely deaths of Black children. It is heartbreaking. I am scared. I am writing this letter to you because I know what the power of determination can do. Because I know you can achieve anything when you put your mind to it.

I will end with the words of Martin Luther King Jr. *"In the end, we shall remember, not the words of our enemies, but the silence of our friends."* I ask you to be a friend to us Black people. Be an ally. Be the change. I know, I am becoming the change that I want to see in my world.

For instance, I never used to speak to any of my neighbors while walking in my neighborhood. But, since this whole quarantine business, I have decided to go out of my way to speak to as many of my neighbors (mostly White) as I can. And these days, I see that they are all just as friendly and as interactive with me as I am with them.

I am therefore, asking you to do your part. Help end the senseless killings and barbarism. Help end racism and discrimination. Martin Luther King Jr. had a dream, let's help make that dream come true. It is indeed long overdue. He put it so aptly when he said, *"Injustice anywhere, is injustice everywhere."*

As you read these words, I hope and pray you open your hearts. I hope you look into the eyes of your children and see your future generations and the continuation of your lineage. I know that deep in your heart, you only want what is best for them, much like I do. I want you to know that after all's been said and done, I am just a mother who wants her babies to come home each day at sunset, to her warm embrace.

"The only way, to really talk about race and racism, is by activating a growth mindset." ~Amber Colemen-Mortely

I say, *"the only way to really talk about race and racism, is to freakin' talk about it."*

Cheers!
Your Friend and Coach,
Uchenna L. Umeh, MD, MBA

Appendix I

Kobe Bryant. In full Kobe Bean Bryant, (born August 23, 1978, Philadelphia, Pennsylvania, U.S.—died January 26, 2020, Calabasas, California), American professional basketball player, who helped lead the Los Angeles Lakers of the National Basketball Association (NBA) to five championships (2000–02 and 2009–10).

Ahmaud Arbery. On February 23, 2020, Ahmaud Marquez Arbery, an unarmed 25-year-old African American man, was fatally shot near Brunswick in Glynn County, Georgia, while jogging. Arbery had been pursued and confronted by two white residents, Travis McMichael and his father Gregory, who were armed and driving a pickup truck. The event was recorded on video by William "Roddie" Bryan, who was following Arbery in a second vehicle. The death and events following the investigation have sparked debates about the lack of racial equality and have been reported internationally.

Breaona Taylor. On March 13, 2020, Breonna Taylor was shot to death by police in her own home. In what is being described as a "botched raid." Officers barged into her apartment in Louisville, Kentucky, as she lay sleeping in her bed and fired multiple rounds into her innocent body.

Christian Cooper. A Black man who had the New York police called on him, by Ms. Amy Cooper. He is a Harvard graduate, a former Marvel Comics editor and now the senior biomedical editor at Health Science Communications. Amy was recorded by Christian after he simply asked her to comply with New York City law and put her dog on a leash.

George Floyd. George Perry Floyd Jr. (October 14, 1973 – May 25, 2020) was an African American man killed during an arrest in Minneapolis, Minnesota. Protests in response to his death, and more broadly to police violence against black people, quickly spread across the United States and internationally.

Amazon is an American multinational technology company based in Seattle that focuses on e-commerce, cloud computing, digital streaming, and artificial intelligence. It is considered one of the Big Four technology companies, along with Google, Apple, and Microsoft. It has been referred to as "one of the most influential economic and cultural forces in the world" as well as the world's most valuable brand. You can find Dr. Lulu's books in her author page on Amazon at this link: https://amzn.to/2NcklkH

Race. A race is a grouping of humans based on shared physical or social qualities into categories generally viewed as distinct by society. The term was first used to refer to speakers of a common language and then to denote national affiliations. By the 17th century the term began to refer to physical traits.

Trayvon Martin. Trayvon Benjamin Martin (February 5, 1995 – February 26, 2012) was a 17-year-old African American from Miami Gardens, Florida, who was fatally shot in Sanford, Florida by George Zimmerman. On the evening of February 26, Martin was walking back home, alone from a nearby convenience store.

Sandra Bland was a 28-year-old African American woman who was found hanging in a jail cell in Waller County, Texas, on July 13, 2015, three days after being arrested during a pretextual traffic stop. Her death was ruled a suicide, but new evidence tells a different story...hmmm.

Post-Traumatic Slave Syndrome. P.T.S.S. is a theory that explains the etiology of many of the adaptive survival behaviors in African American communities throughout the United States and the Diaspora. It is a condition that exists because of multigenerational oppression of Africans and their descendants resulting from centuries of chattel slavery. A form of slavery which was predicated on the belief that African Americans were inherently/genetically inferior to whites. This was then followed by institutionalized racism which continues to perpetuate injury.

Persistent Traumatic Stress Disorder or continuous traumatic stress is a term that was originally developed in the 1980s by a group of mental health professionals working in apartheid-era South Africa. They were attempting to provide psychological support to victims of political violence within a context of ongoing state repression.

Continuous traumatic stress offers one possible way of describing the psychological impact of living in conditions in which there is a realistic threat of present and future danger, rather than only experiences of past traumatic events. It foregrounds the difficulties of addressing past exposure in the context of an accurate appraisal of the potential for current and future harm.

Post-Traumatic Stress Disorder. Post-traumatic stress disorder (PTSD) is a mental health condition that is triggered by a terrifying event — either experiencing it or witnessing it. Symptoms may include flashbacks, nightmares, and severe anxiety, as well as uncontrollable thoughts about the event. If the symptoms get worse, last for months or even years, and interfere with your day-to-day functioning, you may have PTSD.

A Teen's Life, Dr. Lulu's second book. Written in a "Dear Doctor" format, this book chronicles the lives of 12 fictitious teens from across the globe. It focuses on childhood trauma, and its effects on suicide. It explains how each teen navigates their struggles and arrives at various life-altering decisions. Grab your copy on Amazon. Type this link in your browser: https://amzn.to/2NcklkH

JAMA Pediatrics: The pediatric division of the Journal of American Medical Association. It first published the study on Black children and their suicide risk.

The Washington Post. Published the article about African American children and their suicide risk which is twice that of their White counterparts. The study was done from the year 2000 to 2015, and the result was replicated in other studies. Overall, between 1999 and 2015, more than 1,300 Black children ages 5 to 12 took their own lives in the United States, according to the Centers for Disease Control and Prevention. Those numbers translate into an average of one child 12 or younger dying by suicide *every five days*.

My Blog is called Words by Black Butterfly. You can find it at www.wordsbyblackbutterfly.com

Niecy Nash. Carol Denise "Niecy" Nash is an American comedian, actress, television host, model and producer, best known for her performances on television. Nash hosted the Style Network show Clean House from 2003 to 2010, for which she won an Emmy Award in 2010.

Wyt-Fear: 1844WYTFEAR is the fun number Niecy suggests you call ☺.

Amy Cooper is a White woman who called the police on Christian Cooper, a Black man and bird watcher in Central Park, New York. This was after he simply asked her to leash her dog. The video has since gone viral, and Ms. Amy Cooper has been fired from her place of work. Ms. Cooper lied on the 911 call and accused him of 'threatening her."

Nkpokiti. (Aka Mkpokiti)_*Mkpokiti* as a Nigerian national dance. *Mkpokiti* represented the federal government of Nigerian in FESTAC '77 at Lagos. In New York, Washington, Jamaica, Barbados, Brazil, Venezuela, Trinidad and Tobago, Cuba, Port of Spain, and England, *Mkpokiti* dance has been exhibited as the greatest cultural dance in Africa. The Satinsheen Company under the management of Miss Franca Afebua took *Mkpokiti* dance to a global competition in Wembley, England. All the groups competed in Oxford University, England. *Mkpokiti* dance secured the 1st prize there and carried the World Cup back to Nigeria. The achievements made in these travels including winning the World Cup multiple times even in New York, Algeria and North Korea a few years ago rightly crowned the legendary *Mkpokiti* dance of Igbo people the greatest cultural dance in the world.

Breakdance. Breaking, also called **breakdancing** or **b-boying /b-girling**, is an athletic style of street dance from the United States. While diverse in the amount of variation available in the dance, breakdancing mainly consists of four kinds of movement: toprock, downrock, power moves and freezes. Breakdancing is typically set to songs containing drum breaks, especially in hip-hop, funk, soul music and breakbeat music, although modern trends allow for much wider varieties of music along certain ranges of tempo and beat patterns.

Soul Food is an ethnic cuisine traditionally prepared and eaten by African Americans in the Southern United States. The cuisine originated with the foods that were given to enslaved West Africans on southern plantations during the American colonial period; however, it was strongly influenced by the traditional practices of West Africans and Native Americans from its inception. Due to the historical presence of African Americans in the region, soul food is closely associated with the cuisine of the American South although today it has become an easily-identifiable and celebrated aspect of mainstream American food culture.

Implicit Bias. Also known as implicit social cognition, implicit bias refers to the attitudes or stereotypes that affect our understanding, actions, and decisions in an unconscious manner. These biases, which encompass both favorable and unfavorable assessments, are activated involuntarily and without an individual's awareness or intentional control. Residing deep in the subconscious, these biases are different from known biases that individuals may choose to conceal for the purposes of social and/or political correctness. Rather, implicit biases are not accessible through introspection. The implicit associations we harbor in our subconscious cause us to have feelings and attitudes about other people based on characteristics such as race, ethnicity, age, and appearance. These associations develop over the course of a lifetime beginning at a very early age through exposure to direct and indirect messages. In addition to early life experiences, the media and news programming are often-cited origins of implicit associations.

Conscious Bias. The second type of bias identified in the literature. In the case of explicit or conscious, the person is very clear about his or her feelings and attitudes, and related behaviors are conducted with intent. This type of bias is processed neurologically at a conscious level as declarative, semantic memory, and in words. Conscious bias in its extreme is characterized by overt negative behavior that can be expressed through physical and verbal harassment or through more subtle means such as exclusion.

Appendix II

Action Points

21 Day Challenge

Visit: https://www.teenalive.com/21-day-challenge.html

1) Listen with an open heart. Don't feel a need to share your own story at this time. Just listen.

2) Be open to the discomfort you feel, don't discard it, acknowledge it.

3) Don't take it personally. No one is blaming you as an individual. Don't make this about you.

4) Develop some emotional intelligence about this topic, control your negative reaction when discussing this topic.

5) Breathe.

6) Be supportive of your Black and Brown friends whenever you can.

7) Come to terms with your implicit biases and get training on it.

8) Become aware of any stereotypes about the Black community that you have.

9) Get some trauma-informed training, most cities are offering those now.

10) Be present, be intentional, and be mindful of your interactions with people of color around you.

11) Be an advocate for your children's Black friends by including discussions about race in your spaces.

12) Normalize the conversation of race in your home and place of work.

13) Apologize, if, and when you get an opportunity to do so.

14) Notice racism and call it out, then work towards stopping it.

15) Address explicit biases around you, and the systems you support.

16) Question the stories you have been told about Black people as you were growing up.

17) Stop supporting or funding the "school to prison" pipeline.

18) Donate to bail funds and pro-Black Lives Matter operations.

19) Hold space for your Black friends.

20) Support Black-owned businesses.

21) Give yourself some grace and compassion.

Type this link onto your browser for a downloadable PDF
https://forms.gle/wuHqVK5Yf4J93hhL7

About the Author

Uchenna L. Umeh, MD, also known as Dr. Lulu a.k.a. The Momatrician is a board-certified pediatrician and a mom of *trés hijos* (her three wise men). She is an award-winning bestselling author of "How to Raise Well-Rounded Children," and "A Teen's Life." A former lieutenant colonel and commander in the United States Air Force. She is a TEDx Speaker, United Nations Speaker, Global Pan African Speaker, and Youth Suicide Prevention Activist. She is Nigerian born, a proud Igbo woman who speaks 8 different global languages. She is also the CEO of Teen Alive, and Dr. Lulu's Youth Motivational Space, both dedicated to the care of youth dealing with trauma, stress, anxiety, overwhelm and suicidal ideation. Connect with her at teenalive.com, youthmotivationalspace.com, uchennaumeh.com, or call (802) 768-1180.

Next Steps

Did you enjoy reading this book?

Answer:

What are *your* thoughts?

Answer:

Did this book change your perspective?

Answer:

What are your top 3 takeaways?

Answer:

Are *my* thoughts valid?

Answer:

Are my suggestions practical and "easy" enough?

Answer:

Are they thought-provoking?

Answer:

What emotions are you feeling right now?

Answer:

Do you think you will carry out the commandments?

Answer:

Which of them are the most challenging and why?

Answer:

Would you recommend this book to a friend or family member?

Answer:

Who?

Answer:

Can you start a reading club with others who have read this book?
Answer:

I encourage you to start the conversation amongst yourselves. Light the spark… Be that change. Become an ally. That would mean so much to me, my sons, and the Black race.

I am a parent and youth motivational, book-writing and speaking coach, I would love to connect with you, or anyone you know that might need my services.

Do you need a coach, or a speaker for your next event?

Send your request and responses to these questions to: askdoctorlulu@gmail.com

Lastly, would you please write an honest review about this, or any of my other books on Amazon?

That would really help get my books in front of more awesome readers like you, as you stay tuned for my next book, "What if My Child Is a Bully?" It should be dropping fall of 2020. I look forward to sharing it with you as well.

Thank you,

Dr. Lulu ☺

CPSIA information can be obtained
at www.ICGtesting.com
Printed in the USA
LVHW090731020221
678031LV00005BA/1227

9 781733 751254